PURE L
AN INTRODUCTION TO WESTERN PURE LAND BUDDHISM

Jim Davis

2005
EKO Publications
Springfield, MO

(c) 2005 by Jim Davis

PURE LAND NOW!
AN INTRODUCTION TO WESTERN PURE LAND BUDDHISM

Jim Davis

EKO Publications
PO Box 603
Springfield, MO
65801

from_alamut@yahoo.com

AN INTRODUCTION TO WESTERN PURE LAND BUDDHISM

The purpose of this text is to provide a brief introduction to the teachings of Western Pure Land Buddhism.

What is Western Pure Land Buddhism?

Western Pure Land Buddhism (WPLB) is the name I have given to the latest development of the Mahayana Pure Land tradition. It shares with all other Buddhist groups the ideal of attaining Nirvana, not just for oneself, but also for all beings. Thus the goal of one's life is to realize Buddhahood in order to help others see this world of birth-and-death as Nirvana. Where WPLB differs from most other Buddhist is in teaching that Buddhahood is a gift to us from Amida, the Buddha of Infinite Light and Life, and that we return that gift by the saying of Nembutsu (Namah Amida Buddha).

From where did Western Pure Land Buddhism originate?

The teachings of WPLB ultimately derive from the teachings of Shakyamuni Buddha who lived in Northern India over 2500 years ago. Now Shakyamuni Buddha taught many teachings, but few understood them. So before his Paranirvana (his return to Mythological reality) he taught the Three Pure Land Sutras in order to enable all people, especially those unable to take the path of monk/nunk-hood, to return with him into Nirvana. Then his lay followers traveling the worlds' trade routes spread the teachings throughout Asia. By the time Buddhism reached Japan it had started to degenerate into a state religion supporting the aristocracy and the rich landowners. Temples even raised armies to attack each other and to put down peasant uprisings. By the 13th century Buddhism had reached a moral low point and it was at this point that reformers appeared. It was at that moment which gave birth to Soto Zen, Nichiren Shu, Jodo Shu and Jodo Shinshu (also known as Shin Buddhism). The Western Pure Land Buddhist teaching owes its beginning to the founder of Jodo Shinshu, Shinran.

Who was Shinran?

Shinran founded Jodo Shinshu, when he made a collection of passages from the Sutras and the commentaries concerning the Pure Land. This collection is called the *Kyogyoshinsho*. It outlines the way to Buddhahood, the Nembutsu and of taking birth in the Pure Land now. Shinran was born May 21, 1173 near the city of Kyoto, Japan. His parents died in his early childhood and he was sent to a Tendai Buddhist temple to become a monk at age eight. Over the next 20 years he spent practicing the methods of self-power (more on this latter) to try and force his way into enlightenment. He suffered a spiritual crisis when he came to realize enlightenment was impossible by his own efforts. Abandoning the temple at age twenty-eight, he met the monk Honen who was then teaching the Other-Power path of Amida Buddha and birth in the Pure Land. Through abandoning all practices and responding to the awakening of faith through Amida's Important Vow (that Amida would not become a Buddha if all human beings who with sincere mind, faith serene, desire birth in the Pure Land and who recites the Nembutsu even just once, did not take rebirth there and achieve supreme enlightenment),[1] Shinran received the certainty of enlightenment (shinjin) as a gift from Amida. Then Shinran spent the rest of his life teaching the Pure Land path to the common people of the land.[2]

---

[1] This is not to imply that the other 47 vows are in anyway lesser to this Vow. It is just that historically this one vow has been seen as pivotal. In this day and age I feel we need to look at the other vows and see how we can apply them to our current situation

[2] Shinran spent most of his teaching carrier amongst the people in rural areas teaching the people of the peasant class. This was in direct opposition to the usual spiritual carrier of great teachers of his time. They would go to the capital and set up teaching members of the aristocracy. Shinran after a life of teaching did retire to the capital to write his books, but did not seek to publicly teach (tho former students did go to visit him and receive teachings).

How did the Pure Land teachings come to the West?

Like all other forms of Buddhism, Pure Land Buddhism arrived through the efforts of the Asian immigration during the late 1800's. Specifically, the Japanese immigration to Hawaii and the West Coast gave rise to the first Buddhist missions. The present organization the Buddhist Churches of America is the main branch of Japanese Pure Land Buddhism in the U.S.

What is the meaning of Other-Power?

Within Buddhism there are two main groups in which the various Buddhist practices are organized. These groups are the paths of self-power and the paths of Other-Power. Self-power paths are those ways (like sitting meditations, koans, visualizations, ritual. etc) in which one tries by one's own will to force oneself into an enlightenment experience. And yet, many of us find that these practices are difficult or impossible for us, as laypersons, to undertake. We have neither the time nor the will to complete them successfully. And unless one abandons secular life and take up monastic practice then one will have great difficulty in following the paths of self-power. Yet we are not without hope, that hope is the Other-Power. Amida Buddha out of great compassion took upon itself all the burdens of practice. The Pure Land Sutras teach that the merits Amida Buddha created by practice are transferred to us as a gift of awakening faith.

Who is Amida Buddha?

Amida Buddha is the Buddha of Infinite Light and Life. There is no place within the universe where the light of the Buddha's compassion does not shine. And through infinite life, there will be no being within the universe left out knowing Nirvana.

Amida Buddha is the universal personification of one's own innate buddha-nature. When awakening arises it is the union of the "savior" (Amida/buddha-nature) and the "saved" (the body). Awakening to the certainty of enlightenment (shinjin)[3] takes place within the body. The body becomes the Pure Land in which Amida Buddha dwells. The descriptions of the Pure Land found in the sutras are symbolic descriptions of the awakening body and its possibilities.

Amida Buddha is not a god. The Buddhas do not have the power to create, maintain or destroy worlds as people have historically envisioned the gods and goddesses doing. It is to free beings from the sufferings of birth-and-death. For the purposes of our daily lives this world is eternal and uncreated. It is

---

[3] A definition first advanced by Radical Shin teacher Ken O'Neill of Austin, Texas.

driven only by the power of karma and constant change.

Amida Buddha is neither a he nor a she. But since we human beings insist on personifications, we can refer to Amida as of either gender. The Japanese traditional address Amida as our father and mother (our spiritual parents).

What is the Vow?

This is the promise made by Amida that all beings that will say its name will be reborn in the Pure Land and quickly achieve enlightenment. This is realized in the present moment through an experience of awakening, the certainty of enlightenment (shinjin). It takes place within this body and within this lifetime.

What is the Certainty of Enlightenment (shinjin)?

This is the single moment of experience in which one becomes personally aware of the reality of one's certainty of enlightenment. It is to be grasped by Amida Buddha's promise, never to be abandoned. It is the point of non-regression; one cannot fall back into a lower rebirth (unless one does so in order to fulfill one's vow to become an Enlightening Being). It is the awakening of oneself through the awakening of all others; the awakening of others through one's own awakening. And it is, the complete equality between oneself and the future Buddhas of all worlds.

How does one practice Western Pure Land Buddhism?

Shinran taught us to view practice as no practice. Other Buddhist groups taught that one had to practice precepts, do rituals, meditations, visualizations, etc., to win Nirvana. WPLB sees the awakening of the certainty of enlightenment as a gift from Amida Buddha and not as a reward for successful practice. Due to past good actions we have arrived at this life and this time. It is this point of time in which we have the good fortune to receive these teachings. We respond to the hearing of these teachings by saying the Nembutsu (Namah Amida Buddha) once. And yet, when awakening arises one cannot keep it to oneself (since one is linked to all) and one goes on to chant the Nembutsu out of gratitude. In the light of this gratitude one may then go on, if one likes, to experience the many facets of Buddhist experience. Thus we can do the other Buddhist practices. If one does not go on to practice other ways, then at least do not slander them. Many come to awakening in other paths; no one has a monopoly on awakening.

How does one become a Pure Land Buddhist?

Becoming a Buddhist who follows the Western Pure Land Path is mostly a matter of self-identification. One may make a public declaration through a public ritual and take the Three Treasures Pledge. After which one then associates with other Buddhists in an organized manner face-to-face. Study groups or basic Buddhist communities could be formed. Be a light onto yourselves, but grow with others. Do not let others dominate you just because they started on the Buddhist way before you did. Remember the teachers you may meet are to serve you and not the other way around! Of course, you will become a teacher of others so keep it cool.

Is conversion the equal to the Awakening to Certainty?

Deciding to follow the Western Pure Land Buddhist way is not the same as awakening to the certainty of enlightenment. This awakening is a personal experience between you and Amida. No teacher or organization can give this awakening (they can only be an example of the possibilities which others have found and wish to share). Also, there is no certification of "enlightenment" as found in some other Buddhist sects. While joining a WPLB group is not equal to awakening, rest assured that all who try to live a life of Nembutsu will awaken in this life and in this body.

What is a life of Nembutsu?

The life of Nembutsu consists of chanting the Nembutsu and teaching others the way. It is to live a life without fear. And to join with others to better achieve these goals.

Should I accept WPLB teachings on faith alone?

No, for we should always test the value of teachings in our everyday life. Shakyamuni Buddha taught the Kalama people, who were being confused by the conflicting claims of roaming religious teachers (very much like today!), to test all teachings first. That is, not to accept a teaching purely on authority, tradition, logic, conformity, faith, etc., rather one should only accept a teaching after first putting it into practice and realizing its truth.

What now?

As of March 2005 there are no national WPLB groups, only individuals trying to put something together. I have been posting this document and others from a now defunct newsletter (EKO) to the Internet in order to prepare the way for individuals to start Basic Buddhist Communities in their own homes. And after practicing in that way for a while a national federation of BBC's may then be formed. I am willing to aide in this effort and to provide information (and to receive it). I can be reached at:

Jim Davis/EKO
P.O. Box 603
Springfield, MO
      65801-0603

The Basic Teachings of Western Pure Land Buddhism

1

This is the Good News of the Buddha Shakyamuni,[4]
a manifestation of the Unhindered Light,[5]
which has come to us from across the centuries.
To take on a new and more Western form
for this New Dharma turning age.[6]
This Good News I first heard from the Buddhist Community,
those who are fellow travelers on our way
and who graciously share their faith with others.
The Community received the Good News from Shinran.
Shinran received and taught
the teachings of the Seven Pure Land Ancestors.[7]

---

[4] This is the historical Buddha who lived in northern India over 2500 years ago.

[5] This is another name for Amida, the Buddha of Infinite Light and Life, who lives mythically in the Western Pure Land.

[6] Refers to the end of "mappo" the last 500 years of a 2500-year cycle of 500-year wheels. We are now at the beginning of a new 500-year cycle of Buddhist expansion.

All of whom,

correctly heard and transmitted

the true meaning of the Pure Land Sutras[8]

as given to us by Shakyamuni 2500 years ago.

Thus I establish these teachings.

---

[7] Usually called patriarchs by those who use poor English. They are: Nagarjuna, Vasubandu, T'an-luan, Tao-ch'o, Shan-tao, Genshin and Honen.

[8] Which are the Larger Pure Land Sutra, the Smaller Pure Land Sutra and the Meditation Sutra

2

The classical Pure Land tradition is based

upon the Three Pure Land Sutras:[9]

the Larger Pure Land Sutra,[10]

the Smaller Pure Land Sutra[11]

and the Meditation Sutra.[12]

And of these three sutras,

Shinran took the Larger Sutra

as his main text,

out of which he expounded

the awakening of enlightenment

through Other-power.

And yet,

Shinran did seek out inspiration in other sutras,

and within

the writings of the Seven Pure Land Ancestors.

So we can also seek out truth in other sutras;

---

[9] These are the three canonical sutras of Jodo Shinshu and most Pure Land sects.

[10] This sutra tells us of the origin of Amida Buddha, expounds the 48 vows and describes the Pure Land.

[11] This sutra describes the Pure Land and the practice of chanting Nembutsu. Due to its shortness it is often used for ritual chanting in it's entirely.

[12] This sutra tells us the story of an Northern Indian queen whose husband had recently been overthrown by his son. In despair she turns to Shakyamuni Buddha who teaches her 16 meditations concerning Amida Buddha. This text has been a basic manual for Pure Land Buddhism until Honen/Shinran began to teach Nembutsu-only.

the Dharma is not bound by three small books.
All the sutras teach various truths
and other great practices.
All of which, if correctly practiced
leads to awakening.

3

This universe of the body is samsara;[13]
six worlds[14] spin about within it.
It is a chaos of birth-and-death
manifesting itself as beginningless suffering.
Birth, illness, aging and death are sufferings.
To be separated from those you love
or to be attached to those you hate,
are both sufferings.
To have what you do not want
or not to get what you do want,
are also sufferings.
The teachings do not deny
that there is happiness.
Yet one should not doubt
that these pleasant states of being are fleeting;
suffering always finds a way back into our lives.
With the passage of time
even our greatest pleasures become boring.
Some feel that death is a way out of suffering.
This is a delusion.

---

[13] Also, referred to as birth-and-death

[14] The six worlds are the realm of the gods, the realm of the anti-gods (Titans), the realm of human-beings, the realm of animals, the realm of the hungry spirits, and the realm of the hell-beings. Traditionally, all six worlds are considered real places, but Japanese Buddhism during the Middle Ages viewed them as psychological states.

Death does not bring an end to suffering
as due to the weight of our deeds (karma),
we take rebirth again and again.
Thus giving rise to a new life of suffering.
This cycle of life-and-death has no beginning,
and if left to itself,
no ending.

4

And yet, hope is never far away.

Long ago,

out of the depths of myth,

as beginningless duration,

birth-and-death became conscious of itself.

This consciousness is the One Mind.

It was moved out of great compassion

for the infinite number of beings

trapped within itself and vowed to save them all.

That consciousness is the Eternal Buddha.

The Eternal Buddha is Amida,

the Buddha of Infinite Light and Life.

One should always remember

that Amida is not a god

nor the creator of this universe;

Amida is neither Yahweh[15] nor Brahman.[16]

This universe has neither first nor last cause.

One does not stand in awe in Amida's Light;

in the light of awaking there can be no fear.

Amida is our eternal friend

who is there always for us

---

[15] This is the name of the original Hebrew God (God-the-Father/Allah).

[16] The Hindu creator God who is generally ignored in Modern Hinduism, but was still a major deity when Buddhism began.

for Life immortal.

5

From time to time
Amida's Light takes human form;
into a world of vast darkness and endless death,
the Eternal Buddha takes birth.
Shakyamuni Buddha is the manifestation,
the essence of Amida's Light and Life to this age.
If one takes on the perspective of passionate beings
trapped within the systems of greed, hatred and ignorance,
then this is a dark age.
And yet, through the great compassion of the Buddha's teachings
Amida's Light and Life,
has reached out to embrace us.
This embracing is the awaking of enlightenment.
It is to be grasped,
never to be abandoned.
Thus Amida's Light dispels forever all dark ages.
Mappo is no more!

6

Shakyamuni Buddha taught all who came to him.
according to their level of understanding.
Traditionally it is claimed
that 84,000 different Buddhist teachings were all
proclaimed by him.
And from time to time,
place to place,
one or another of these many teachings
would come to prominence.
Sometimes even new teachings are remembered[17]
and taught.
As for myself
I follow the Western Pure Land Buddhist path
and hope others will come to benefit
from these teachings.

---

[17] Sometimes those whose prior life had been in the company of the historical Buddha is able, due to good karma, to remember forgotten sutras.

7

In one sense,
Shakyamuni Buddha's advent into this world
was to bring the teachings to you.
Due to the past good of numerous others,
you have now received this good fortune:
this very teaching you are now hearing.
Since this teaching is here
faith can not be far away.
Amida's Light has shone upon us patiently
it is time for us to wake up.

8

Due to beginningless greed, hatred and ignorance
we have all been chained
to the cycle of birth-and-death.
Since we have up till now
failed in all attempts to free ourselves.[18]
Why do we continue to delude ourselves
with thoughts of self-power?
Amida gives us faith in the other-power.
And through great faith
Amida awakens within us the Pure Land itself.
Freedom is impossible within birth-and-death;
bondage is impossible within the Pure Land.
Awakening faith transforms
birth-and-death into the Pure Land.
This gift of faith in awakening enlightenment
has broken down the gates of hell
and its captives have been freed,
now and forever.

---

[18] Some sutras recount individuals who have practiced for numerous kalpas (billions of years) but still failed to achieve enlightenment.

9

Amida's compassion reaches across the darkness of space and time,
to save all beings.
No harmful karma can stand in the way of this compassion;
nothing we can possibly do
can ever separate us from Amida's embrace.
If through past evil deeds,
we cannot help but to break the many precepts,[19]
then we would be forever lost by our own power.
However, Amida over looks our past faults,
converts evil karma into good
and turns this body into the Pure Land.

---

[19] Rules of conduct which if taken too literally makes life dull and boring. The problems with rules and legalism is a problem most religions have had. Mystics in most faiths pass through the level of legalism to a mystical libertarianism.

10

One should always keep in mind
that other Buddhist groups may have many rules,
precepts,
practices,
food taboo's, ect.,
all of which, makes it most difficult
for the layperson's faith to awaken.
And yet, these all are traditional spiritual paths,
many taught by Shakyamuni himself
and therefore we should not slander any of them.
However, that does not mean we have to follow them.
As no single Buddhist group ever tries to practice all of
the teachings,
they pick and choose
according to their times and place.
It is now a new time
and the West is a new place.
It is now the time and place
for a new tradition to emerge.

11

We hear repeated about the need to abandon the ego,
in order to realize liberation,
from all Asian religions.
And the Pure Land sects are no different.
However, to abandon the ego
is to rely only upon the other-power.
How is this possible?
All efforts based upon self-powered acts
only serve to strengthen the ego.
To accept that nirvana has already been given to us,
is to abandon all attempts to force our way in.
It is based upon faith,
and yet,
even this faith is given to us.
We do nothing
but accept Amida's gift.
Just say "Namah Amida Buddha"
and live the Pure Land now.

12

We do not have to go off on great pilgrimages
to India, Thailand, Tibet or Japan,
to hear and receive awakening faith.
When the conditions are right,
awakening takes place in the here and now.
No need to abandon secular life
to enter monasteries
or even take weekend retreats.
This awakening takes place
as we live our daily lives.
There is no longer a false split;
no more sacred/profane dichotomy.
The moment of the awakening of enlightenment seeks
us out
and finds us
wherever we may be.

13

Amida is the result of her Vow.
The Vow that if any living being
calls out her name in faith,
they will take birth in the Western Pure Land.
In her land
all who takes birth there
will become great enlightening beings.
Who then return again and again
to the world of birth-and-death
to save the many beings.
The Vow arose out of universal compassion
which manifested itself as Amida.
This compassion is true and real
and so, are its incarnations.[20]

---

[20] In a sense, all existence except ourselves are manifestations of universal compassion. When we stop seeing ourselves apart from universal compassion we realize the unity of Amida and ourselves. When this is personally experienced we call it the awakening of enlightenment.

14

To say "Namah Amida Buddha" through faith
even just once,
is to break the chains of karma.
It is to be embraced by universal compassion
never to be abandoned.
It is to take birth in her land now;
once has become the equal of Maitreya,
the future Buddha.
This gift of faith has been ever present
but only now have we accepted it.
The past good of innumerable past lives
have finally born fruit
in the awakening to enlightenment in this life.

15

Say the Nembutsu just once through faith
and thereafter only out of gratitude.
One's life itself becomes Nembutsu.
This is the life of faith:
to awaken to enlightenment,
to act justly,
forgo all fear or superstition
and to teach others to do the same.

16

The call of nembutsu
and our response to it,
are both manifestations of the awaking of
enlightenment.
To hear and to receive
is open to all:
female and male,
young and old,
gay and straight,
non-Asian and Asian,
those good and those evil, etc.
When one's inherent enlightenment awakens
all social distinctions are overthrown
in this life and in the next.
Remember if religion can not free us
in the here and now,
how can we trust it in the next life?

17

The awakening of enlightenment is a gift;
it is a benefit freely given to us by Amida herself.
No one can stand between Amida's gift and us.
No one can deny or take back from us
awakening faith through the other-power.
Therefore, be free women and men!
Do not grovel or bow at the guru's feet,
nor do any slavish senseless things
in order to receive initiation or transmission.
All of can receive the Infinite Light and Life directly,
freely and without preconditions
from Amida herself.

18

Many who practice Asian religions
do so to gain great powers or
to have all their desires fulfilled.
Saying Nembutsu,
I have no such powers.
Though I lack them in all ways,
I do not seek them either.
Life is wondrous as it is.
All ways of power I reject!
Since none leads to awakening
seeking such powers
can only lead to more misery.

19

This world of birth-and-death
is Amida's field of action;
Amida has always poured out to this world,
great faith,
so that all can awaken to enlightenment.
She has reached out to us
arising out of the very beginninglessness of existence,
so that today we have the great fortune
to hear and say her name.
And now having been set free
birth-and-death itself becomes the Pure Land.

20

So to conclude,

live your life,

act compassionately,

struggle against oppression

and injustice.[21]

And after the end of this life,

return again and again

to this world,

until every last being

including the grass,

the animals,

the trees

and the land

all enter together into Nirvana.

---

[21] During the Middle Ages in Japan, Korea and Northern China numerous peasant uprising occurred based upon Pure Land ideology (against the state and state Buddhism).

A Commentary on the Five Lay Precepts

So simple and yet so complicated, the precepts have from the very beginning been a source of many problems. Created by the Monastic Sangha, themselves bound to +227 regulations, to give the laity a sense of monastic practice (especially when combined with the three other training precepts) and opportunity to avoid creating harmful karmas. Yet practicing the precepts would not create Nirvana; the best one could hope for was rebirth in a Hindu-style heaven or rebirth as monk/nunk. Most followed the precepts to avoid painful rebirths in the hell-worlds. Given the universal nature of precepts, which are found in all religions, precepts are not a particularly Buddhist practice.

Historically, Pure Land Buddhism has downplayed or outright rejected the use of precepts based upon its concept of Other-Power. However, if the terms of Self and Other Power are seen as ways of going into Nirvana, then the precepts would fall outside of this dualism. The use of precepts has nothing to do with Nirvana; the precepts do not deal with ultimate spirituality. They are instead the way to a good life in this world. So in place of Rennyo's [the sixth head of Jodo Shinshu] rule about obeying the laws of the land. I would advocate using the precepts, while holding society and the State up to its standard. It is in this light that I make this commentary.

REFRAIN FROM KILLING: this means I will not kill human beings.

This means I will not engage in aggression against other people. And yet, I am aware there are times when the killing of other beings becomes necessary and unavoidable. I will protect my own life and the lives of others of whom I find myself karmically attached. I will strive to create a society of peace through justice and convert this society of violence to peace.

This means I will oppose all state violence and executions.

This means I do believe that abortion is killing and that life begins before conception (life is beginningless and endless). And yet, I recognize the samsaric nature of this world of birth-and-death and will not stand in the way creating further suffering. I will struggle against the society of death that causes many to choose abortion as the means to avoid poverty and missed opportunities. I see the only way to do this is to end poverty through full employment, universal healthcare, universal daycare and education.

This does not mean I have to give up the eating of meat. The early Buddhists clearly ate meat and so did Shakyamuni Buddha. Prohibitions against the eating of meat are taboos adopted from Jainism. The logical result of not taking life in the area of food is to choose death by sacred starvation (which is a holy Jain practice). All eating requires that beings die both plant and animal, that is the way of all things. However, we should be mindful of how the food we eat is obtained and to reduce as much as possible the suffering of those involved.

REFRAIN FROM STEALING: this means I will not take what is not given.

This means I will try to stop others from taking what is not given through the systems of exploitation, or economies, based upon greed.

This means I should support the poor and not the rich. I will join movements to end economic injustice.

This means I will join movements to protect the earth from exploitation as to not allow present greed to steal from the future. I recognize other creatures and plants have rights to existence and to their share of the earth's bounty.

This means I will not condemn the poor if they have to break this precept out of poverty.

REFRAIN FROM SEXUAL MISCONDUCT: this means I will respect the relationships of others and will not seek out sexual relations with those already committed to others.

This means I will only have sexual relations with adults in a situation of love and long-term commitments.

This does not mean celibacy or an endorsement of heterosexuality as the "norm." Buddhism has never had a single sexual ethic that transcended time and space. Rather it adopted whatever sexual mores of the lands it entered and changed as the mores changed. I hold that one's sexual orientation has no bearing on practice, as long as, my previous statements are kept in mind and followed.

REFRAIN FROM UNTRUTHFUL SPEECH: this means I will speak the truth.

This means I will speak truth to Power and struggle against its system of lies and deceits, which maintain its systems of poverty.

This does not mean I will have to speak the truth if I feel by doing so will endanger the innocent lives of other beings.

REFRAIN FROM INTOXICATION: this means I will not use chemicals to become mindless.

This means I will struggle against the system which provides the chemicals to make the poor and working classes mindless in order to maintain their power and wealth.

This does not mean I am against the moderate use of alcohol. There does appear to be health benefits from moderate use. As always stick to the middle path between the extremes of indulgence and abstinence.

In conclusion, the precepts are more important as social practice than as individual practice. They are something we try to do for the benefit of others. So while it is true that practicing them will not result in Nirvana, but at least we will not turn this world into Hell.

How to Practice Western Pure Land Buddhism

(basic daily ritual)

The spiritual life of a Western Pure Land Buddhist is a life of gratitude. One of the ways Pure Land Buddhists expressed their gratitude was through a short daily ritual. Within the Japanese lay-oriented Buddhist traditions [from which WPLB derives] this is done twice a day, usually in the morning and in the evening. And yet, gratitude should never be institutionalized or made to be felt as a burden. One may have time for only one round of chanting per day or even week. Whatever practice you can manage for your time is enough. Its not a matter of quantity but of quality.

[standing face the dharma object: a scroll of Nembutsu, picture of Amida or book of sutras]

[raise your right hand in gesture of welcoming]

[light candles and incense]

[sound the dharma bell two times]

[recite the following]

Namah Amida Buddha
Namah Amida Buddha
Namah Amida Buddha

I take my guidance from the Buddha.
I take my guidance from the Teachings.
I take my guidance from the Community.

Through the merits freely poured out to me by Amida Buddha,
may I take birth in the Pure land
and then quickly return to this world
to guide every living being,
including the grass, the trees and the land
into Nirvana.

[read a section from any Buddhist sutra that you like]

I rejoice in the awareness
that Amida's Vow arisen within me.
From beginningless time
Namah Amida Buddha thunders,
but only now have I been given faith to say it.
As this faith infinitely awakens within me

I shall chant:

[chant Namah Amida Buddha as long as you like]

I know, without a doubt
that all who chant the Nembutsu in faith
have the gates of hell slammed shut forever.
To be grasped,
never to be abandoned
is to live life without fear of its end.
I shall chant Nembutsu
and share it with others.

Namah Amida Buddha
Namah Amida Buddha
Namah Amida Buddha

[sound the dharma bell three times]

[raise your right hand in gesture of departure]

[leave]

The End of Mappo

Many people in the West are unaware that Buddhism too is infected with an "end of the world" mentality. It is known as mappo (in Japanese). While not quite the end of the world, it does means the last 500 years of a 2500 year cycle in which the Dharma taught by Shakyamuni Buddha would fade away (and with its resulting evils). This cycle started on the date of the Buddha's Enlightenment experience. However, the dates for the Buddha's life vary so it is difficult to say exactly when this cycle started.

Japanese Buddhists, following their Chinese teachers, believed that Shakyamuni lived about 1000 BCE. Therefore, mappo began about 1000 CE and they read into the events of their times the signs associated with the Dharma decay. This idea of the decay of the Dharma was a major reason for the rise of new Buddhist schools which taught an easy way to enlightenment. The reason for this is that they saw the practices taught by the traditional sutras as too hard for people living in mappo.

The problem with mappo is that it should be over, but Japanese and other Buddhists just will not give up this doctrine. By any calculation, the last 500-year period should be over (whether your take the Chinese date or the modern scholarly date of a 5th century Buddha). You will find the date for mappo extended from 500 years (which is what the Lotus Sutra taught) to 10,000 years which commentators on the sutras claimed. People appear to want to be living in "a last age" and will do anything to do so.

However, the Lotus sutra did not actually saw that the Dharma would completely decay. In the 23rd chapter it advocated that Buddhists should spread it thruout the world, lest that the Dharma be lost. This implies that maybe if the Lotus sutra was spread thruout the world then the Dharma would not fade away. And this is what actually occurred. At the time when the Dharma was at its lowest point (last century), the Dharma (including the Lotus Sutra) came to the rest of the world (The Lotus Sutra itself was translated several times and placed in universities around the world). Its been in a state of renewal ever since. So mappo is over and its time to get out of the gloom of the last days. So while the Lotus Sutra is strangely silent on what comes after mappo, it is apparent that we are living in a new exciting time of the Dharma's renewal (a fourth turning of the wheel?).

One's Mind is the Buddha

Pure Land Buddhism has often been compared to Christianity and Amida Buddha was see as a "Buddhist God." Toss in confusion about the meaning of Other Power vs. Self Power, and its no wonder that many see no difference. Since many Westerners have rejected Christianity they see no reason to adopt what they see is a Buddhist Christianity. This is truly sad since I feel that Pure Land Buddhism has much to offer the average layperson living in the West. It is more suited for the average person than say Zen or Tibetan Tantra. In fact, the vast majority of Mahayana Buddhists practice some form of Pure Land faith. This has not been the case in the West, tho things are beginning to change. I will be writing a series of short essays on various topics which I feel is important to understand Pure Land Buddhism in the West.

One of the things one needs to get straight right away is that Amida Buddha is not a "god" out there. Amida Buddha is the Eternal force of Life and Light who has arose out of the beginninglessness to guide all beings into enlightenment. Mythologically, Amida does this by bringing all those who call Amida's name into the Pure Land where the conditions are so right that enlightenment is assured. Tho it really still is up to us to do the work necessary for emancipation. Many feel that this Pure Land is after death like the Christian heaven. No, it is this body that is the Pure Land and it is the Mind that is Amida. As the Contemplation Sutra teaches: "Your mind produces the Buddha's image, and is itself the Buddha." And before we get too egotistical here, one needs to remember that there are no individual minds in Buddhism. All minds are One Mind and that Mind is the Buddha. It is only as the result of past karma and present delusions that cause us to see ourselves differently.

A PURE LAND TEACHING

for Today
I

We base these teachings upon the Three Pure Land Sutras and the Lotus Sutra. Further we accept Shinran's [founder of Jodo Shinshu in the 13th century] writings, tho we interpret them in the context of a new cycle [post-mappo]. Tho we base our faith upon the interpretation of these sutras, we, in no way, abandon the other sutras nor urge others to abandon their sutras or practices. They are all Shakyamuni Buddha's teachings and practices.

There are two gates of practice: the gate of expedient practices and the gates of essential practice.

The gate of expedient practices include the practices of precepts, vows, zazen, insight meditation, visualization, chanting sutras, study, debate, etc. All of these are good practices and thru them Amitabha, the Buddha of Infinite Light and Life, leads beings to the certainty of enlightenment. These are all difficult practices and some are not for everybody. Yet Amitabha gives power to those who feel called to perform them. If this were not the case, then the words of the Buddha would be untrue. Since the various sutras all teach various ways to enlightenment, Amitabha helps all who undertake them.

The gate of essential practice is to remember the name of Amitabha Buddha. Traditionally this is done thru the chanting of Amitabha's name [which varies according to the language of the people] and in the Jodo Shinshu tradition is the Nembutsu. This remembrance is complete with one utterance and any chanting afterwards is done out of gratitude for the sake of others. Thru this remembrance Amitabha transfers power to us and awakens within us the certainty of enlightenment [shinjin].

Some people feel called to a mixed practice. They perform expedient practices and the essential practice together. While others take up the essential gate and perform expedient practices out of compassion for others. Thus assisting others on their chosen path manifesting the power of Amitabha' compassion.

Our goal is realization of nirvana in living itself. Whether one practices expedient or essential practices the end result is the same: a personal gnosis of one's fundamental unity with Ultimate Reality. Once this experience arises, one does not wait to engage in bodhisattva deeds. Spreading the teachings of the Buddha throughout the world, the world itself becomes the Pure Land. And then, after one's passing from life to life, returning again and again to this world to assist in the freeing of all beings [including the land, the grass, the animals and the trees] from the delusion of living in samsara. Thus all shall find themselves as complete nirvana.

THE FOUR RADICAL TRUTHS

Out of the beginninglessness of space and time arose COMPASSION. Viewing the many worlds of woe filled with innumerable suffering beings COMPASSION was transformed into Amida (Amitabha), the Buddha of Infinite Light and Life. And in order to relieve the suffering of human beings in this world system, Amida became the Enlightened One, Shakyamuni Buddha, over 2500 years ago in Northern India. Being fully and completely human, the person who was to become Shakyamuni Buddha experienced the full gamut of pleasure and pain. Only when he abandoned self-power practices of asceticism and sought the middle path did COMPASSION transform him through an experience called enlightenment. After which he went out into the world to each the many so that they could overcome suffering and become Nirvana.

All Buddhist teachings flow from Shakyamuni's experience of enlightenment and are the means in which beings use to share in it. This is the path away from existential suffering and meaningless existence. Shakyamuni first organized the teachings into the form of the Four Radical Truths. This is also called the middle path and all further Buddhist teachings can be seen as commentaries upon this basic system.

The first Radical Truth is the truth of suffering: birth is suffering; aging is suffering; illness is suffering; death is suffering; the presence of things we hate are suffering; separation from things which we love are suffering; not to obtain what we want is suffering; and to obtain what we do not want is suffering. In brief, all existence is suffering. This view does not deny states of happiness and bliss. Only that all such states are by their very nature fleeting and elusive. Samsara is the name given to this state of universal being; it is the world of birth-and-death as it is. Death results in birth and birth in death; an endless cycle of life, death and rebirth. Thus birth-and-death is a prison of beginningless suffering. And yet, it is also the site of great opportunity. As only in the here and now of this world due we as conscious beings have the possibilities of breaking our chains of bondage and together enter into Nirvana.

This is the Second Radical truth concerning the origin of suffering: suffering originates in that craving which causes rebirth, it is accompanied by sensual delight and seeks satisfaction now here, now there; that is to say, in the craving for existence and for non-existence. As we all are driven by the force of our former deeds (karma) birth-and-death continually arise; deluded we go on to pour even more gas onto the raging fires of samsara. Thus suffering gives rise to suffering until we come to the time where we start to look for a way out of this beginningless inferno.

This is the Third Radical Truth concerning the cessation of suffering: it is the mindful cessation without trace of craving; the laying aside of, the giving up of, the being free from, the harboring no longer of, this craving. This state is called Nirvana; it is the suffering being's experience of unity with COMPASSION.

This is the Fourth Radical Truth concerning the path, which leads to the cessation of suffering (the transformation of samsara into Nirvana): it is the Radical Eightfold Path, that is to say, right views, right intent, right speech, right conduct, right means of livelihood, right endeavor, right mindfulness and right meditation.

This is also called the Way of the Middle path, which goes between the extremes of spiritual practice of asceticism and hedonism.

Every Buddhist sect teaches a path, which has its basis in these four truths, even tho, may use different words and concepts to communicate the teachings. Each group has taken up the Radical

Eightfold Path in its own way. And now that Buddhism is taking root in the West it is struggling to create a new synthesis with Western culture. It is time for new and different Buddhisms to emerge. It is to this spirit of emerging Western Buddhisms that I make this version of the Radical Eightfold Path. The basis of this view is Pure Land Mahayana Buddhism and Western prophetic thought.

The Radical Eightfold path is:

RIGHT VIEWS: This means to embrace the Buddhist teachings with the intent of putting them into practice. Mere belief is not the Buddhist way.

RIGHT INTENT: This is to have as the sole aim of our practice the goal of liberating all suffering beings from the net of samsara. It is to vow to lead all beings, including the grass, the trees, the animals and the land, into Nirvana before our own entry.

RIGHT SPEECH: To speak the truth so that our words correspond with our deeds. Avoiding speech tho factually true which harms others and to oppose lies of the ideologies of materialism.

RIGHT CONDUCT: To strive towards keeping the basic precepts as much as our self-nature allows and to apply these principles to our society at large. To actively participate in the social movements to stop warfare, state executions, animal torture, state secrecy, economic exploitation, the misuse of sex by advertisers, and the use of drugs in a policy to destroy the poor.

RIGHT LIVELIHOOD: To follow and choose an occupation that does not contradict one's commitment to the Buddha's teachings. Specifically, we are to avoid those occupations, which involve the killing of human beings.

RIGHT ENDEAVOR: To constantly strive to realize the Buddha Way despite the obstacles which arise (and you know you are on the right path when they do arise). Thus one converts all Maras one encounters into great teaching Buddhas.

RIGHT MINDFULNESS: To use the various practices as a means towards increasing awareness constantly striving to see samsara as it really is.

RIGHT MEDITATION: In the Mahayana Pure Land tradition this means to respond to the gift of awakening faith, to come to hear, to say the Nembutsu, and then to chant thereafter out of gratitude.

So this is the basic teaching from which one can go on to develop an ever-increasing Western Buddhist movement. We should not hesitate to be imaginative in the creation of this New Buddhism. This task has already begun.

GATHAS TO PROCLAIM WESTERN PURE LAND BUDDHISM AS I TEACH IT

While there are many different Buddhist practices,
I simply chant the nembutsu.
Yet because others take up other practices
I compassionately assist them in their chosen way.

While the universe has been fucked up from its "beginning,"
I simply chant the nembutsu.
Only in this way can I end the exile
leading all beings back into Nirvana.

While many teach we are evil beings,
I simply chant the nembutsu.
Seeing instead the fundamental goodness of others,
I shall do my best in responding with gratitude.

While others proclaim we are basically evil,
I simply chant the nembutsu.

Since the historic Buddha taught that the world is what we think,
I now know how to transform the world.

While many believe we are living in the last age,
I simply chant the Nembutsu.
As the wheel of Dharma has seen many turns,
I now see a new turning of the wheel.

While many selfishly keep the Dharma treasures to themselves,
I simply chant the nembutsu.
And out of deep gratitude for my own ongoing awakening,
I seek out opportunities to share Amida's gift with others.

While many seek awakening in far away lands,
I simply chant the nembutsu.
Awakening to the certainty of enlightenment is not the monopoly of Japan or Tibet,
the place where one sits
and chants is the Pure Land.

While many shame themselves
by fawning after gurus,

I simply chant the nembutsu.
Receiving awakening directly from Amida herself,
I bow down neither to gods nor masters.

While many seek initiations from gurus and lamas,
I simply chant the nembutsu.
As the certainty of enlightenment flows from Amida
there is no need for human intermediaries.

While many bow to images or teachers,
I simply chant the nembutsu.
Since Buddhism is not a religion of submission,
I choose to stand or sit instead.

While many offer ritual acts to images,
I simply chant the nembutsu.
Since neither Shakyamuni Buddha nor any of his early followers used images,
I choose to abandon all appearance of idolatrous activity.

While many import Asian deities into the West,
I simply chant the nembutsu.
I we must use deities, then let us use the deities of Europe and North America,
to act as the protectors of Buddhism in the West.

While many feel it is important to create a monastic oriented Buddhism in the West,
I simply chant the nembutsu.
Realizing that historically the Dharma has always been spread and supported by the laity,
I call into question the value of monasticism.

While many Buddhists dialogue with Christianity,
I simply chant the nembutsu.
Personally feeling that Christianity does not connect with my Euro-American based collective unconsciousness,
I choose to dialogue with neo-pagans instead.

Shinran on the Gods and Goddesses of the Land
(based on the Genzeriyaku Wasan)

When one chants Namu Amida Butsu,
Woden (Brahma) and Thunor (Indra) pay homage
and all the good sky gods
will protect them day and night.

When one chants Namu Amida Butsu,
all of the gods of goddesses of Asgard together
will protect them day and night,
keeping evil trolls and dark elves away.

When one chants Namu Amida Butsu,
the Vanir (gods of earth) pay homage.
And just as the shadow pursues the object,
they will protect them day and night.

When one chants Namu Amida Butsu,
the Light Elf King and his army of elves
pay homage to the devotee
and will protect one day and night.

When one chants Namu Amida Butsu,

The goddess Hel pays homage
and together with the lords of the nine worlds,
will protect him day and night.

All the gods and goddess of MiddleEarth and Asgard
should be called good deities.
Together these good gods all
protect the person of nembutsu.

The faith of incomprehensible vow-power
is the great mind of Enlightenment.
The evil trolls, dark elves
and giants which lurk on earth
all fear that faith.

from:
Foundations of Japanese Buddhism Vol. 11
Alicia & Daigan Matsunaga
pp 107-8

Printed in Dunstable, United Kingdom